WICCAN SPELLS

Step-by-Step Guide To Wiccan Spells

Lisa Buckland

TABLE OF CONTENTS

CHAPTER 1

WICCAN SPELLS

When we think of the word 'magic' our mind automatically drifts to the movies. We visualize someone holding a wand or some other apparatus, saying something we don't understand, and pointing. Just as that is done, a bright beam of light emerges out of the instrument, causing something quite impressive. But here is where we have accepted an imaginary phenomenon, one which has grown in to a stereotype. Magic is not a make-believe act, performed for the entertainment of the crowds.

Another misconception that prevails in our minds is that magic is done for personal gain. Few of us know that some kinds of magic are performed for a religion belief. Such is the case with Wicca.

Wicca is a religion and a form of modern witchcraft. It finds its roots in Paganism, a religious movement which came into existence hundreds of years ago. Wiccan spells are also referred to as 'Magick', to try to differentiate it to the type of tricks used by performers to entertain during their shows.

Wiccans adhere to some basic principles, and abide by them while casting spells. The most important one is to do no harm. Magick must only be used for the betterment of the people. They also believe that whatever actions you do in life, come back to you with three times the intensity. Many Wiccans also consider mirth, reverence, honor, humility, strength, beauty, power and compassion as the eight virtues of life. They respect the five elements of the world that is earth, fire, water, air and spirit. This is why the pentagon, a symbol of the union of those elements, is of great importance to them. And contrary to beliefs, they are not Satan worshippers!

Wiccan spells are used to invoke the powers of the God (called the Horned God) and Goddess (called the Triple Goddess) to bring about some positive change, fulfill desires and solve problems. The phase of the moon is tracked as it is important for the specific spells to be successful.

Spells are a part of the Wiccan rituals of religion. The most common sort of Wiccan spells that are performed are ones to get rid of negative energy, to rise above illness, and for good luck and protection. Most of the spells are followed as they were originally written, but many like it better if they can modify it, making it a lot more personal.

Most people find the power and intensity possessed by Wiccans and their spells quite intimidating. However, they don't realize the purity of their acts. They don't understand that these spells are a way of making a connection with nature, and sending out some positive energy.

HOW TO CREATE YOUR OWN WICCAN SPELLS

One of the many questions neophyte practitioners put forth is, "how do I create my own Wiccan spells?" While there are many books offering a variety of spells for personal use, some practitioners prefer to write their own. In doing so, you empower spells with your personal intent, thereby making them far more powerful than a spell taken from a book that doesn't evoke the emotional response or seriousness of intent needed for a spell to prove successful.

If you find spells that you have become somewhat fond of, but you would feel a lot stronger about them if you could just "tweak" a few things, you can use spells offered in books or online. As you adapt spells to suit your personal preferences there are several things you'll need to consider. First and foremost, remember that if you are adapting spells from other works, your adaptations are for your personal use only. A lot of pagan writers offer spells for adaptation, but you definitely don't want to infringe on the copyright of authors or online writers by sharing your adapted works online or off, especially without the consent from the original authors of the adapted work.

Before you begin writing or adapting spells at all, make sure you think about what it is that you really want; "watch what you wish for" is implied here. Make sure you are clear about, not only what you want, but why you want it, and how you expect your desires to manifest. You should also give full consideration to any and all potential outcomes of your magickal workings; sometimes when you are working magick you can end up with a result that gives you precisely what you asked for, but not necessarily the way you expected. This is why specificity is so important to the working.

Whether you are adapting spells you have become fond of or writing your spells from scratch, you'll need to keep your intent in the back of your mind. Every word in the spell needs to align with your intent and the desired outcome. To that end, how specific you are with your spells will define the success of your spell casting endeavors. To lend to the specificity in your writings, you can perfect the wording and timing of the work and you can make use of magickal correspondences.

Timing - Some practitioners time a spell working during a specific moon phase. For instance, you can time spells during the waxing, full, or waning moon phase. The waxing moon is associated with beginnings and the waning moon with endings, while the full moon is associated with all magickal workings. So, if you are conducting a spell where you want a situation to end, you can time your work for when the waning moon appears, and if you are looking for a new start in a situation, the waxing moon is the most ideal time to perform your work. Some practitioners also time their work based on days of the week, the season, the planetary hours, or according to astrological correspondences.

Rhymes - Not all spells rhyme, but you might find that you are far more comfortable working with rhyme. You'll find it easier to remember and when using rhyme you create a rhythm with your words when spoken aloud. When you write your own spells, you should spend some time memorizing what you've written. This way you can give your full attention to what words you are speaking instead of reading them from a piece of paper.

Visualization - Your spell should contain precise wording that will not only help you verbally express your desires, but you'll also want wording that triggers your visualization abilities. The more intensely you can visualize your desired manifestation, the greater the likelihood you will achieve the outcome you seek. In fact, before working a spell, it's a good idea spending some time visualizing your desired outcome. As with your spell's wording, when visualizing you need to be as specific as possible, seeing your desired outcome in every possible detail.

Positivity - Finally, if you're a Witch practicing the Wiccan religion, you'll want to make sure that your spell's wording and intended outcome is aligned with the Wiccan Rede of, "harm none, do what ye will." As a Wiccan practitioner, you should be concerned with the Threefold Law of Return and the potential backlash that accompanies the act of sending out negative energies. Make sure your spell workings are positive so that what comes back to you in the way of manifestation is equally positive.

HOW TO SET UP YOUR WICCAN ALTAR FOR THE FIRST TIME

Wiccan altars are a very personal affair. What you decide to keep on yours will be down to what you feel gives you energy and the tools that you have a connection with. After that of course, you will want to lay out tools or items that you are working with for a particular spell.

That said, some items and layouts are traditional and if you are setting up a Wiccan altar for the first time it would probably be wise to follow a few basic 'rules' until you find you own way. Here are some of the core principles:

- Energies are often divided into masculine and feminine, especially Gods and Goddesses. You may have icons pertaining to a particular deity on your Wiccan altar, or it could be your tools (e.g. your Athame is considered masculine) so you should place the feminine objects on the left side and masculine on the right.

- You should view your Wiccan altar as the embodiment of the core elements of earth, air, fire, water and the spirit. Your altar should enable you to connect with yourself and the world around you on a profoundly spiritual level. To represent the elements you should have salt for the earth, candles for fire, a chalice or bowl for water and a feather or incense for air. People have individual preferences for their representations, but make sure that you go for symbolisms that speak the loudest to you.

- Your altar should be at waist height. You need to be able to use it with ease and without obstacle.

- Avoid clutter. This will distort the flow of energy on your altar and you will not be as efficient. It is more common for altar tables to be round shaped as this helps with ease of movement for circular rituals. Casting a circle is not essential but many prefer the reassurance of having a 'scared' space in much the same way as worshippers feel safe and protected in church. However, if space is your main issue then it is fine to have a square table.

- Your Book of Shadows is of course essential to your spell work, so it should be placed in the centre in order for you to both work from it and also to make notes as quickly as possible to avoid forgetting any important details.

- When you are setting up a Wiccan altar for the first time, or using new tools you will need to consecrate them. This is a very important procedure and not to be skipped as you will be recharging the vibrations and energies. To consecrate the area try smudging which entails burning sage around the area. You may wish to prepare a chant for the occasion. Smudging will also work for tools and is certainly a quick and easy way to do it. However, there are many other options available to you including sprinkling your tools with salt water or even submerging them overnight if possible. Once again, this is a matter for the individual so go with what you feel drawn to.

- Place something personal on your newly set up Wiccan altar. This is because at first it may all seem a little strange and unfamiliar to you which in turn will hinder your energies and make your spell work less effective. Arrange something personal to you on your altar somewhere, particularly something of sentimental value. Consider it to be a bit like taking a friend along to somewhere you've never been before! It won't be long until your altar and tools will become as one with you and you will not need this extra item.

HOW TO APPLY WICCAN SPELLS AND CHARMS

When there is so much energy all around us, do we really need anything else to bring in that extra bit of luck to our lives? Yes, to derive the best from nature and to bring added luck to your life, we may need to accumulate our inner energy to revitalize our inner self.

The very word "spell" reminds us of the several fairy tales that we have heard from our childhood days. The story of the prince who turned into a frog was quite popular then. The needle on which the spell was cast to prick and make the princess fall asleep for years and many more such stories which dealt with spells were quite familiar.

On the other hand charms are mostly defined as some magical objects which can bring good luck. A doll in some mythical story given to a little girl by her mother on the death bed, showered in luck into the girl's life. She was saved from every uncanny situation. Her stepmother was the witch.

Yes, Wiccan spells and charms not only bring luck and fortune in the lives of the fairy tale characters, but also in our lives. Ranging from spells of broader categories like money, love, etc. to simple categories like: your pet's health, helping grow more plants in your garden, growing slim, keeping young etc, these spells find a prominent place in quite a number of individuals' lives.

Wiccan charms on the other hand are some beads or amulets which are assigned to perform certain tasks in your lives bringing in that extra bit of luck. A youth charm can help maintain youthfulness and a health charm can look after your health.

But performing of Wiccan spells and charms are not so easy. Observing certain rules is a must. Not abiding by these codes can bring in misfortune and sometimes can cause a spell to bounce back quite adversely.

Using the Wiccan spells and charms to bring in bad luck for some person or to dominate someone without their wish is strictly prohibited by Wiccan spells and charms. Thinking wisely and measuring the pros and cons of spells or charms are what all the Wiccan spell and charm performers are expected of.

The Wiccan spells can sometimes be very simple, comprising of just a bit of a phrase or a line maybe, but again it can be very complicated. Some spells are supposed to be conducted during specific time of a month to complete a full cycle.

To get the best results and to keep evil out and bring in luck, several magical objects can be used. But, then again the ways of placing the objects, the directions or other instructions if prescribed are suppose to be followed very accurately.

The only problem we can encounter when all this is not followed. This may result in the occurrence of a back spell. Wiccan spells and charms with its sheer glory are bound to shine over our lives with luck only, when done with utmost care and patience

CHAPTER 2
WICCAN SPELL CASTING TECHNIQUES

Wicca is an age old pagan religion which deals with various spell casting techniques and crafts. There are many activities that we do and find our friends and relatives doing, which actually their origins have deeply rooted in Wiccan art and spell casting techniques.

From childhood days you have found yourself blowing candles while making a secret wish during your birthdays. The technique of blowing out candles has their origin in Wicca. There are many candle involving spells which you will find greatly used in Wicca for the purpose of solving health and love related matters.

Apart from these there are many other techniques of spell casting which we unknowingly use in our day to day life.

There are special colors of candles that are put to use for achieving various purposes of spells. White candles are meant to invite positive and white forces in your life and bring in good luck. Orange candles are used for the sake of creating opportunities in your life. The uses of green and pink candles have got to do with wealth and love related issues.

And lastly, black candles can be used to ward off negative forces. Many people have a wrong notion that black candles can come to use only when one chooses to work with dark forces or rather black magic. But Wiccan spell casting techniques have nothing to do with black magic and its philosophy has always been of live and let live. So there are no chances of dark energy dominating any of the spell casting techniques.

Wiccan spell casting techniques always teach that one should clear his or her conscience before working with any kind of spells. You should not give shelter to any kind of negative vibes, desires or trepidations while working with the spells. Since Wiccan spells have got to do with positive energies, the workings of these spells get highly meddled if any of your negative emotions come in between. The results can never be satisfactory if the positive energies involved are disturbed.

Lastly it is always advisable to prepare the appurtenances that are required for the spell by you to yield best results. By producing them all by you, will ensure that your true passions and feelings are playing a dominant role during the spell casting technique. If that is not possible then ensure that you are using fresh things, which have not been used by any other person before you.

KEY POINTS TO MAKE FREE WICCAN SPELLS WORK FOR YOU

1) Pre-written free Wiccan spells will get you started but they will not teach you the way of Wicca so be realistic in what you aim to achieve and in your expectations of how successful you can be at first.

2) You will need ingredients and tools although you do not always have to shell out on an altar and the accompanying equipment in the first instance. Bowls, a sharp implement for carving or other makeshift implements will do. But you should aim to represent the 5 core elements of Wicca - salt for earth, incense for air, a candle for fire and a goblet or bowl of water (for water obviously!).

3) The words in your chosen free Wiccan spell are not necessarily the most important thing. It is the belief, the energy and the spirit behind it - this is the life-force behind your spell work. If you are merely reciting words or scribe then expect nothing. Your spell is no more likely to come alive then reading aloud makes characters in a book come to life. It is all in your ability to connect with the powers of the elements and spirit around you and within yourself. You will begin to learn what feels right and what feels flat.

4) However, some of the free Wiccan spells out there have been written with an energy and a feeling folded in to the very words themselves, showing that the author had a passion about their spell work. If you are picking up on this and feel excited by the spell then there is no reason that it wouldn't be able to work for you.

5) Go for spells that you feel drawn to and can identify with. That almost feel a part of you.

6) Avoid bad spells, hexes or curses or the Wicca (Rede) threefold law will come to pass. Whatever energy you put out there into the world around you, you can expect back but 3 times as powerful so be responsible.

7) Most Wiccans and witches will go through a preparation ritual in order to get themselves into the right frame of mind for performing their spell work and you should do the same. It can be something as simple as a scented bath or practicing some meditation but try to get yourself into a relaxed and open state.

8) Do obey any extra instructions that come with your free Wiccan spell, such as seasonal time restrictions or the cycle of the moon. These influences on the spell are there for a reason so don't try to get away with short cuts.

9) You may be looking for old and ancient free Wiccan spells and they certainly carry with them power that has accumulated over the years. But bear in mind, the language can be difficult to understand and interpret so make sure you fully get the meaning. Not all are genuine either so research them thoroughly!

10) Start simple. There is no point in trying to jump in at a higher level than you are ready for. You will be wasting your time and risk doing more harm than good.

11) Start a journal/book of shadows for yourself and write your free Wiccan spell in it for future reference. Write notes of what happened and any observations that you may have had. This way, when you are more experienced, you may be able to come back to this spell in the future and adjust elements to suit your needs.

TOOLS YOU WILL NEED FOR MAGICAL AND WICCAN SPELLS

If you are new to using Wicca and magick spells or know things already you will learn from this article. I would like to share some tips on what to use as tools and devices for your practice of the occult arts.

All of these ritual and spell items you can find in stores or online. You may not agree with my tools or ritual items, but I can guarantee through my own experiences they do work. Here are my best key notes from what I know works best for Wicca rituals and magick spells.

1. Magick candles - To set the mood and have a power like the element of fire is very positive and powerful when conducting a ritual or casting a Wicca spell. The element of fire is one of the four magickal elements that make our universe and make Wiccan rituals and spells work. As an example, you can write down on a piece of paper while in a self-induced hypnotic state, all of your fears, anxieties and worries.

Next thing to do is pray for them to be healed through the light and fire of the candle and set the letter ablaze. Be sure you have a bowl of water to put the flaming paper in. This is a great ritual magick technique that works to remove depression, stress and toxic energy.

2. Magick Tarot Cards - Being able to see your reality and lifestyle objectively through the lenses of your higher self is amazing. This is why and how tarot cards are used. Out of 72 cards, each card embodies a different archetypal energy we as humans go through in life.

The use of tarot cards can provide you with insight within yourself to greater depths. Tarot cards can also give you the advantage of knowing what the day has planned for you ahead of time. I highly and sincerely suggest that you buy a deck of your own cards for best results.

3. Magick Pendulum - A simple and very accurate technique for receiving, yes or no answers to questions can be done with a magical pendulum. You can buy them online or find them in Wiccan and witchcraft shops. I suggest you find a crystal that suits your needs and attach a string to it.

To use this you hang it above a piece of paper divided into two parts. One saying, yes and the other no. Whichever way your pendulum swings will give you the answer to your question.

WICCAN CANDLE SPELLS - THE TECHNIQUE

Wiccan Candle Spells have been used since a long time to bring forth your wishes. The Wiccan Rede states, "And it harm none, do what thou wilt". This means that you should not harm any person or living being.

The Threefold Law states, "All good that a person does to another returns three fold in this life; harm is also returned three fold." When it comes to magic spells candles play an important role in a lot of religions. The Wiccan magic spell is not different.

But colors of the candles have an important role to play too. This means that the color of the candle will depend on the desire of the person who is doing the spell. For instance, if you want prosperity and luck with sudden changes, you will use an orange candle. If on the other hand, you want financial benefits along with fast luck, you should use a gold candle.

Financial success and money are attracted by brown candles while good fortune, prosperity, money and financial issues are brought together by the green candle. Purple candle is used for ambition.

For use in magic spells, homemade "beeswax candles" are recommended. You can however add magical carvings and additional oil to the candles. It is also recommended that you use only one candle per magic spell. Do not put the light out but let it go out naturally.

How you decide to work with your candles is up to you. You can make it ornate or simple though it will depend on the ritual. In fact, the Wiccan candle spells can also be combined with other ceremonial or popular magic for some occasion. You can also practice them alone in the sanctity of your religious space. The ingredients which you need for Wiccan candle spells are the following:

• Color candles, depending on what you desire

• Kind of Oil to use on candles

• Magic Signs cut on the candles

• A Divine Energy needed to light up a candle

• Grass to disperse at the bottom of candles

If you do not want to use magical characters or herbs in your candles you do not have to. A lot of witches use dried herbs to place their candles. However if you want you can make the Wiccan Candle Spell very detailed and complex. For this you have to match colors of the candle with divine energy or force and aromatic oils. You have to match all of this according to astrological calculations.

When you are casting a magic spell, there is a limit to the number of days you can cast them. They are generally cast for nine, five or seven days. If you want the spell to stay for a longer time, you have to light a certain number of candles every day for some time.

A fully fledged ritual can be created when you are doing this spell. There is no limit to your creativity with the Wiccan Candle Spells.

CHAPTER 4

SPELLS YOU NEED TO KNOW

THE WICCAN LOVE SPELL - DOES IT WORK?

A Wiccan Love Spell is very powerful, effective and forceful - that is why Wiccan Love Spells are so much in demand. Wiccan Love Spells, like any other magic love spells, can help to smooth out the troubles in an existing relationship or can deepen the love and passion in a relationship stuck in the doldrums or it may attract you love from a stranger.

Following are a few very effective Wiccan Love Spells that you should cast to get true love. These spells will work wonders and will also enhance commitment and happiness in a relationship with a named lover. But you have to use a Wiccan Love Spell with extreme caution as, lack of genuineness/seriousness and sincerity of feelings/wishes can have an adverse effect.

Wiccan Love Spell for attracting love

To remove hurdles and obstacles that prevent being eyed out by a wonderful lover and to open out your heart, you can use this simple Wiccan Love Spell. This magic spell has to be performed in total tranquility after creating the necessary time and space.

It involves taking an herb scented shower or bath. You have to first pour sufficient amount of rose essential oil over natural sea salt or bath salt. Take a handful of bath salt. Then you have to run the hot bath. Mix in the water with the salt and essential oil mix. Listen to inspiring music while enjoying your relaxing bath. Now you have got to dress up in clean clothes. Wear your favorite outfit.

Then light scented or aromatic candles and incense and arrange multi colored flowers to facilitate the arrival of a new lover in your life. Create a Wiccan altar by placing a clean piece of cloth on table. Then arrange pink or red flowers on this altar. It is best to go for scented roses. Then you have to arrange 4 red or green candles in 4 corners of the altar in each cardinal direction - west, east, south and north. If colored candles are unavailable, you may safely use white candles.

On the altar, you have to next place 1 piece of rose quartz.

Take a suitable container and burn love incense in it. Place the container on a charcoal disk. Some of the ideal herbs are frankincense, lavender or rose or you may settle for a store bought mix of love incense.

Then you have to loudly declare your heartfelt desire for love with full sincerity. Speak in a language in which you are most comfortable. Then you have to meditate for a few minutes. After your meditation is over, you should extinguish the incense and candles.

This Wiccan Love Spell will bring a wonderful lover into your life.

SPELL FOR ATTRACTING ROMANTIC PROSPECTS

This simple spell will put a strong force of Magick Energy at work for you, even while you sleep. Your belief, desire, and focus will be set to work to influence your fate - bringing romantic prospects to you one after another, until a connection is made.

It is a very easy Wiccan spell, but...

Don't let its simplicity fool you - it works extremely well as long as you are familiar with all of the techniques I have shown you previously in this book.

First, of course, prepare your external sacred space, and cast your Magick circle around your altar. Then...

On a Thursday during a waxing Moon, in the first hour after sunset:

Light a purple candle and place it before a bowl of water.

Hold a mirror up to the candle, the water, and then to your face. Gaze into your own eyes. Concentrate on your beauty, your lovability, and your desirability.

Hold the mirror up to the candle again.

Say Aloud:

"In the grace of the universe

And in the abundance of love,

I affirm I am greatly desirable

And open to the bounty of love around me.

The flow of love, romance, and partnership is ever abundant,

And in line with the greater good, I create and attract romance."

With your fingers, put water on the top of your head, in your mouth, and on your heart center. Blow out the candles.

SPELL FOR A LONG & HAPPY RELATIONSHIP

When you have found someone special, someone you are falling in love with - this spell will increase the bond between you and that person.

It does not "force" the bond, but rather magnifies each of your good qualities so that the other can see them more easily. Once everything good about you is magnified, the other person naturally grows more and more fond of you.

First, of course, prepare your external sacred space, and cast your Magick circle around your altar. Then...

On a Friday during the third hour of darkness:

Place a potted cyclamen in the room, and water the plant.

Light three candles: deep red purple, and white.

Say Aloud: "I ask the goddess Branwen to bestow

33

True love on my union with (insert name)."

Breathe your love into your heart. Place the red candle in front of the other candles.

"I ask that this be done for the greater good/

So be it.

And so it is."

Gaze at the flames in each candle, and when you are ready, blow them out.

Love Magick Summary

Remember that it is important for you to be grounded in the basics of Magick and Witchcraft before you attempt any serious Love Magicks. Because desire and emotion are tied so strongly to Love, the spells can have some unpredictable results if you haven't practiced the basic secrets of real Witchcraft.

WICCAN LUCK SPELLS

Have you been down and out on your luck recently? Are you going through a really bad phase in life? Is nothing in your life going in the right direction? Do you feel lady luck has abandoned you for good, leaving you in the lurch? Welcome to the world of Wiccan Luck Spells. With the help of Wiccan Luck Spells, you can reverse your fortune, earn luck and prosperity and success and make lady luck smile on your benevolently once again. Following are a few Wiccan Luck Spells that you may use.

Luck spell # 1

This spell can be used to bring about a metamorphosis in your situation. Choose a Friday evening. Sharp at 7 in the evening, you shall have to burn 7 white candles. Now get hold of a pot of soil. Plant a shorter sized candle in the soil. Let the 7 white candles burn for 10 minutes and then blow them out one by one. The shorter candle should burn till it gets extinguished by itself. This spell, if performed with all your heart, can change a bad situation into a good one.

Luck spell # 2

When you want to bring prosperity and good luck to your home, you can perform this simple magic. Just keep a small package of alfalfa stored away in one corner of your cupboard. That is all.

Jar of luck

Breaking a mirror is supposed to be unlucky and is said to bring 7 years of bad luck. If you accidentally break a mirror, don't worry. Take a glass jar, collect all the pieces of the broken mirror and put them in the jar and keep the glass jar standing on your window sill. The shards of glass, catching the sun rays, have the power of deflecting every bit of bad luck away from your home.

A mantra for well being and good luck

"To the moon. To the sun. To the skies. To the waters. Stars let your fire burn. Winds let your strength grow. Let us unite. Let me shine bright."

Wiccan Luck Spells and charms

When you wish to possess good luck, take a bath in laurel leaves. Or you may create a tiny mojo by mixing together equal parts of patchouli, geranium leaves, laurel, lavender and pine needles. You have to keep this mojo beneath your pillow. Spreading coins and candies throughout your house and in the corners of the rooms especially, can help bring you luck. You can wash a coral with coconut water or holy water and wear it to bring luck. You can also wear orange colored stones that are looked upon as the sun's symbols and are believed to attract luck into life.

SIMPLE WICCA SPELLS TO MAKE YOU SUCCESSFUL IN LIFE

Everyone wants success. That is already a given. But the trick is finding it, or, for it to find you. If you want to succeed in life but you don't know where to start AND you just happen to be just a little bit spiritual, may I suggest that you try several Wicca spells to help get you started. Wicca spells have allowed many a great people find success in life. Good karmic spells allow good positive energies to surround the caster as he/she invokes the power of the spell. If you are new to this, you don't have to worry. These spells are very simple but it can drastically change the way you think and do things.

A lot of Wicca spells offer the caster certain attributes and qualities up until the spells last. Some enable the caster to see inanimate objects or spirits as what some would say. There are other more fantastic spells that are out there like the ability of flight and of an out of the body experience. Today though, we will start with some very simple Wicca spells to help you achieve greater things in life.

Before you continue, be reminded that for Wicca spells to work, you must clear your mind of any negative thoughts. Thoughts of violence, revenge, vandalism or theft will just not work. Focus only on what is good.

Wicca is a branch of witchcraft that was not meant to inflict harm on anyone or anything. In fact, majority of Wiccan practitioners follow the Wiccan Rede - it is a structured guideline on what can and cannot be done with Wicca spells. The Wiccan Rede has but one very fundamental law: do what you want, just don't harm others.

SPELL OF WISDOM

For this spell, you will need a table, a chair, and an object of focus (an old book). Leather bound if possible. First, place the book on the table in front of you. Have a seat, and cross your feet.

If you are a leftie, the left foot should be in front, and if you are right-handed, the right-foot should be in front. Now concentrate your mind on the book and most importantly, keep your eyes on it. As you begin to concentrate, chant the following verses:

"Concentrate myself on the things above and learning all the things I love.

Wisdom be my guide. Knowledge be my guide. Your Spirit be my guide."

Of course, the effects of the spell will not be realized until you apply it to something. Try studying after casting the spell. You will find that learning will come so much easier.

SPELL OF HEALTH

It is best to invoke the Wicca spell of health during the morning just before breakfast. For this spell you will need to brew a potion. Don't worry, there are no cauldrons involved here - not yet anyway.

Here are the ingredients of the health potion:

- 1 cup lemon juice

- 2 cups drinking water

- 1 tablespoon brown sugar

- 1 gram crushed moringa leaves

- 1 tablespoon virgin coconut oil

- A small sprinkle of mint

To prepare the potion, just mix all of the ingredients together in a standard mixing pot and once prepared pour the mixture in a cup or a glass. Before drinking the potion, recite the spell:

"This day I live on given time, to You I give oh most divine

For health and strength to live this day; may Your spirit be mine"

After casting the spell, drink the brewed potion, and that's it! The spell should allow you to feel a lot healthier the rest of the day. Also, as a side note, Wicca spells like these are rare because it can be done on a daily basis. It will be really beneficial and healthy to the spell caster.

WICCA SPELLS TO STRENGTHEN YOUR LOVE LIFE

When you want to strengthen your love life, nothing can be better than taking the help of Wicka Spells or Wiccan love spells. Here are the top 3 Wicka Spells to fortify your love life.

These Wicka Spells are simple and easy to perform, they are delightful to boot and will enhance tenderness and passion in a relationship without freaking out your beloved who is, perhaps, not used to the Wicca way of life.

Wicka Spells # 1

This spell involves performing the ritual along with your lover. The two of you have to bathe together in a bath tub and splash around in water scented with herbs. Take a pestle and grind together sandalwood, patchouli and rose petals and mortar.

Now place the ground stuff in a tiny cheesecloth sachet. Now place the sachet in a hot tub of water and wait for the bath water temperature to reach the optimum level.

Now you two have to bathe together. Gently wash each other with the scented water. No spell can be as magical and passionate as this.

Wicka Spells # 2

When the two of you together eat delicate and exotic small dishes made out of magical herbs for love, it can rapidly and effectively enhance your love life. Some of these food items are a dish of fresh strawberries and raspberries with cream; apple juice or cider; a spicy curry cooked with ingredients like cinnamon, coriander, cardamom and chili.

Another way to spice up your love life through Wicka Spells is to use colored candles during this spell. Orange denotes attraction; pink is used to denote affection, green stands for love while red is universally used for passion.

Wicka Spells # 3

The following Wicca love spell is known as the path of love. When your need is for deep genuine love and you don't want to limit yourself only to desire, you can try this out.

Pick 5 red roses from gardens. Now from your home you have to walk further off. If you travel quite a great distance, you will be able to cast a wider net. You then have to drop down the 1st rose on the ground. At the same time you should chant:

"This is the path of love. My true love will find me."

Continue strewing roses on the ground and chanting this mantra. Be careful to see that you drop the last rose on your door step.

Conclusion

Wicka Spells have their limitations as well. Influencing someone else's free will or causing distress and harm to others through Wicka Spells is strictly forbidden. Because there is this Wiccan Law of Return that ensures that you receive triple the blow that you deal to others as the negative energy gets tripled and rebounds on the individual who practices it.

MONEY SPELLS AND LUCK MAGIC

How do they work? Are they real? If you think of the work "luck" you think of the possible chance that things can go your way for the good. If you are "Lucky" then you often encounter things that maybe bring happiness, money, fun, success etc. The question is there truth to the term "lucky?" Are Money Spells real and how is luck involved. The fact is Money Spells and Luck are both very much related.

Have you ever noticed how certain people seem to have all the luck? No matter what they do they seem to win and win again. They are considered "Lucky" Let's think, what IS luck? Luck is actually a form of attraction magic that ANYONE can have and use. Some people are born with it and others acquire it through various means. Yes, Money Spell or Spell casting IS a way to surround your life with Luck Energies.

EXAMPLE: When a person is confident and simply believe they are going to do well, more often than not, they do very well. This attitude or frame of mind actually creates Luck Magic and therefore radiates it. When this magic and energy radiates it attracts more of it. This is called the LAW OF ATTRACTION.

The Law of attraction is very simple. It states that whatever you put out into the world will come back. This law is universal within almost all faiths and beliefs. The Law of attraction has a very strong magic and mystical foundation. Another fact is that is grows like a snowball. The more you believe you are lucky the more your luck grows. I'm sure you know many people like this. They may even seem arrogant.

Money Spells and Money Spell Castings work in the same way but they use a shortcut. They infuse you with these very energies that attract more of the same luck. This is why when you have a Money Spell cast, a success spell cast, a happiness spell cast etc. The Spell Caster will tell you to believe in the Money Spell and have faith in it. If you have a Luck Spell cast, the directions will be the same. To believe and have faith in your Money or Luck Spell is to make it grow and "snowball" When this happens, money and luck are attracted into your life very fast.

The same holds true for people who have bad luck. I'm sure you know people who seem cursed and no matter what they do it goes wrong. I'm sure you hear these people say "I can never win!" or "Ill never have anything!" They are basically reinforcing the law of attraction and are attracting ONLY negative things into their life. What you say and what you believe WILL become reality.

So, if you have a Money Spell cast or a Luck Spell Cast be certain to believe in the casting 100%. This means more then you know. Also, be very careful with what you say about your own life. Energy flows where attention goes and thoughts become things. Remember those two rules when you desire luck, success, fortune or a Money Spell.

LOTTERY SPELLS TO MAKE YOU RICH

Lottery spells can bring in a lot more than just money; they can bring you a lot of happiness as well. The fact is that the magick in these spells bring luck and charm to the user. The magick lies in the energy that these lottery spells bring into effect. The point remains, while choosing a lottery ticket, that the user needs to concentrate on the flow of energy through his hands and not through his eyes or ears. Lottery spells guide the hands of the person in selecting the correct lottery ticket.

There are three lottery spells that are the most popular among the proponents of magick. Magick can be used to work miracles in your life, it can be used to bring happiness and joy in any form, whether it is money that is required.

1. Candles of green and white color are used in casting the following lottery spell:

"Money, money comes to me

In abundance three times three

May I be enriched in the best of ways

Harming none on its way

This I accept, so mote it be

Bring me money three times three!"

Candles of these colors could be used in trying out the magick. The green color and the green candle is symbolic of money, what you want. The white color and the white candle represent you as an individual. The candles should be anointed with oil before anything being done with them.

2. A lot will depend whether you have a full-moon or a half-moon in the skies when you use spells as the ones given below. A full-moon warrants a lottery spell that involves you in saying

"Lady of luck come out of your hidden course

bless your light upon me as the light of the moon shines above

and in the light of luck will be blessed I, when the moon is next to be full."

3. The moon's brightness has been compared with the color of silver and has always been equated with precious metals. The power of silver is invoked when you say

"Lady of luck come out of your hidden course

Bless your light upon me as the light of the moon shines above

And in the light of luck will be blessed I, when the moon is next to be full."

The spell requires some amount of preparation. For the magick to be effective and the lottery spell to work, you need to fill your cauldron half way with water. Dip a silver coin into the cauldron and move your hand over the surface of the water. This could be symbolic of gathering the moonlight that could be said to be symbolic of silver and money. It is popularly believed that a lottery spell is absolutely compulsory to win a lottery. One is not likely to win a lottery if one does not invoke the supernatural using lottery spells.

These lottery spells could be bought from any of the several web sites offering such spells for some money.

SPELL TO ATTRACT MONEY

On your alter place a green candle in the center. To the right of the candle, place a twenty dollar bill. Between you and the candle, place a piece of pyrite or fool's gold. To the left of the candle place your incense burner with a piece of charcoal in it. When ready to start the spell, light the charcoal and the candle and place basil on the charcoal.

Chant the following while holding the amount of money you want in your mind.

Give me money to live comfortably

Bring enough money to me

I need money to bay what I'm longing for

And I could use even more

I am a good person, I deserve this money

So my life will be cheerful and sunny.

A SPELL FOR HAPPINESS

Collect three chords of thin string, one black, one blue, and one purple. While thinking about happiness, tightly braid the three chords together. Firmly tie a knot near the end of the braided chord while continuing to hold positive thoughts of happiness.

Tie six more knots in the string while still holding the positive energy and happiness thoughts. Carry the chord with you until happiness is abundant in your life. Then place the chord in a safe place or offer it to one of the elements and burn it. Then scatter the ashes in a river or stream.

FOUNDATIONS OF A HAPPY HOME BOTTLE SPELL

This spell's intent is to bring happiness to your home and house all year round. It's is called a cornerstone witch bottle. The definition of this is a witch bottle can be temporary – like to draw new friends or lovers – but a cornerstone witch bottle has the intent to permanent work its magic. You'll touch it up and return it to its place, like the cornerstone of a house. If you move, you will leave the bottle there.

You'll need:

- Dirt or dust from the four corners of your property or home.
- Bottle or jar (any kind)
- Calendar of some kind
- Dried citrus rinds
- Dried flower petals, preferably in yellow, orange, light pink, or other bright cheerful colors
- Sand
- Rice (any kind)
- Flour (any kind)
- Quartz crystal small enough to fit into the bottle
- Wishes for happiness (optional)

First, gather dust or dirt from the four corners of your property. If you home has wonky corners or edges, go ahead and collect some dirt or dust from there too. It doesn't have to be much.

Fill a small to medium sized jar halfway with sand, rice, and flour. Use less flour than rice or sand. Now add in your dirt or dust. Then the quartz crystal, citrus rings, and flower petals.

If you have something specific that you want to brig happiness to your household that year, write it on a piece of paper and include it in the jar as well. This wish could be something like "I want us to be safe and secure" or it could be "I wish for more joyful laughter in our house".

Seal up the jar. You can just twist the cap tightly or use a wax or tape seal. Up to you. Remember that you will need to open this jar again so don't be too aggressive with it.

Bury the bottle somewhere memorable but as close to the foundations as possible. Under the steps, in a flower pot, under the third zinnia. Whatever. You get the idea. Somewhere close to the base of the house. If you live in an apartment, you can totally do this too. Leave the jar in the back of a bookcase or shoe rack near the front door. Whatever you select, it should be as close to the ground as possible.

Mark the date. Make it a reoccurring Google date on the computer, set it up on your phone, and circle it in red on your calendar.

In a year, dig it up, pull everything out, and bury all of it except the quartz crystal. Was and cleanse the quartz crystal. Let it dry completely and repeat the spell, using the same bottle and same quartz crystal. Repeat annually for best results.

Note:

You can absolutely use plastic jars or bottles for this spell.

TRAVEL PROTECTION SPELL

Travel Protection Spell - This powerful magic spell is good for protection during any kind of travel, whether it is a short jaunt or a long distance excursion.

You will need:

- A white feather (a small one is best)
- A bowl of spring water
- Four beeswax candles
- A compass (if you are unsure of where north, east, south and west are located)

Place the four candles on a table, one at north, one at south, one at east and one at west. Spread them out so you have some room in the center. Place the bowl of water in the center of the candles. Dip your right index finger in the water and touch the north candle on its side, dip your finger again and touch the south candle, then the east and finally the west. Next light the candles in the following order: west, east, south, and north. As you light the candles, repeat the following words:

With this flame, I call upon the spirits of the (whichever direction candle you are lighting).

When all the candles are lighted, place the white feather into the bowl of spring water and with it; stir the water in a clockwise direction for about one minute. Remove the feather from the water and wait until the water stops moving. When the water stops, repeat the process of stirring the water, only this time in a counter-clockwise direction for about one minute. Remove the feather and hold it above the bowl in the center of the candles. Repeat the following words:

Spirits of the winds empower this symbol and watch over the traveler who carries it.

While still holding the feather in the center of the candles, extinguish the candles in the following order: north, south, east, and west.

Always carry the feather when traveling.

FINANCIAL PROTECTION SPELL

Financial Protection Spell - A powerful magic spell to protect your money and finances.

You will need:

- One small coin
- A beeswax candle
- A bottle cap, into which the coin will fit

Light the candle.

Place the bottle cap and the coin in front of the candle.

Repeat the following words:

Spirits and guardians of the riches of the world, I beseech you to visit upon this place at this time.

I beg you entertain my plea for protection of the little that I have gained through honest labor.

Remember me in times of financial trouble and strife and guard over my holdings as if they were your own.

This pittance I offer to seal my promise of faith and as a reminder of the one who has called you and requested your favor this day.

Take the candle and drip some wax into the bottom of the bottle cap. Then place the coin into the melted wax. Next, fill the bottle cap with wax, so that the coin is completely sealed in the wax-filled bottle cap.

Extinguish the candle and then break it. Hide the bottle cap in a place where no one will ever find it. Make sure it is in a secure location.

HEALTH PROTECTION

An excellent bath spells for the protection of one's general health.

You will need:

- A beeswax candle
- A sprig of fresh Rosemary
- A sprig of fresh Rue
- A small saucepan or pot
- Spring water

Place the Rosemary and Rue in the pan or pot and add the spring water.

Bring the water to a boil and then remove the pot or pan from the heat. Remove the Rosemary and Rue from the water and discard.

Draw a warm bath.

Light the candle. Place it near the bath.

Pour the water from the pot or pan into bath and stir in a clockwise motion with your right hand.

Repeat the following words as you enter the water:

Spirits of health, spirits of the Earth, water and sky. Bring to me your strength. Give me health and watch over me. Grant me refreshment when I tire and rejuvenation in my weariness.

Bathe in the water.

HOME PROTECTION SPELL

Protection of a Home Spell - An excellent powerful easy to cast magic spell for protecting a home.

You will need:

- A glass bottle (such as a wine bottle)
- A cork to stop the bottle
- Spring Water
- Three pinches of ordinary salt
- Three cloves of garlic
- Three bay leaves
- Three pinches of dried fennel
- Three pinches of sage
- Three pinches of anise
- Three pinches of white pepper

Fill the bottle full with spring water.

Begin adding the ingredients, one-by-one.

With each ingredient that you place in your bottle, repeat the following words:

(Name of the ingredient) which protects, keep my house and all that is there safe from harm.

Repeat the incantation for each ingredient. Once that it is finished, firmly stop the bottle with the cork and shake vigorously for about one minute. Hold the bottle in both of your hands and repeat the following words:

By the capacity of these substances, I entreat protective energies of all that is good to keep my house in security. By this be made.

Hide this bottle carefully so that it is not disturbed.

This spell can be repeated as needed.

FAMILY SPELL

Spell for Protection of the Family - This unique and powerful magic spell is used to protect all members of a family.

You will need:

- A beeswax candle
- One fresh leaf (from any plant) for each member of the family
- One straight pin for each leaf
- A small bowl of spring water

Light the candle.

Place the leaves in the bowl of water and allow them to soak.

Repeat the following words:

As the circle of life springs forth from the Earth and returns to be born once again, so let the circle of life surround this family.

One at a time, remove a leaf from the water, roll it up and stick a pin through it so as to keep it rolled. As you insert each pin, repeat the following words:

Enter (name of a family member) into the circle

Repeat this process until all leaves have been used and/or all family members have been named. Next, place the rolled up leaves around the base of the candle to form a circle. If there are only two members of the family, place both to the right of the candle.

Repeat the following words:

Protect this family

Immediately extinguish the candle. Do not touch the leaves until the candle has cooled. Once the candle has cooled, place one of the leaves under each of the family member's beds.

BRING BACK MY LOVER SPELL

This spell can be used to bring back a former lover or end an argument between friends.

Elements: two white candles on a picture or drawing of your lover or friend to ensure he/she is alone in the photo of a smiling photo of yourself a bag of chamomile tea a piece of blue cloth.

Time: 8:00 am, just the night.

Ritual: exactly at 8:00 pm to light the candles and take a few deep breaths to relax.

Try to imagine a peaceful environment, somewhere beautiful and wonderful.

Now relaxed, keep the image of the person's hand and

Repeat these words:

"to light the flame I'll light your desire, when I speak your name, you will feel my fire, and the die is cast for her!"

Say your name slowly 3 times before you put your picture face down on top of its order that the two images are together.

Wrap the two images, with blue fabric bag.

Put the package in a safe place.

To make sure your ex gets the message to candles at 8:00 each night and says his name three times.

Wait three weeks and it's done.

HOW TO CAST ABUNDANCE SPELL

In our culture, we treat money as an object to possess, opposed to an energy that is shared. From the mystic's perspective, money—like everything else—represents a process, and not a finite substance. We're encouraged to indulge in anxiety about having enough money, and we connect our bank statement to our value as human beings. Unfortunately, this can make money an endless source of anxiety.

When we realize that money is simply energy, then we can really start working our magic – and the best and simplest money magic spell is generosity. The act of sharing what you have—especially when you have little—will generate financial energy that must karmically return to you.

The sages teach that there is no separation between yourself and others, that we are all one, different fingers on the same hand. Seen this way, giving to another is the same as giving to yourself, not because of a future karmic reward, but because giver and receiver are one.

Something as small as offering a homeless person change, or handsomely tipping the cab driver. These small acts inform the Universe that you are a giver, an active participant in the circle of sharing, so the Universe will continue to share with you.

Remember that the Universe is a mirror, so if you are fearful there's not enough in spite of all the abundance in the world, if you indulge in worrying about money, then your world will reflect anxiety back to you, impoverishing you endlessly.

So start by being more generous – but to do this wholeheartedly, you'll have to also cultivate gratitude. Give what you give to whomever you want as an offering of gratitude to the forces that have birthed and sustained you thus far. If you're feeling poor, broke and abandoned by the money gods, remember all the free air you've breathed your whole life, the free sunshine that fills the sky every morning, the free water that falls from the sky. Remember and feel some gratitude. The more gratitude you cultivate, the more your world will give you blessings to be grateful for.

But sometimes you need to bring out the big guns! Whether foreclosure is looming, job prospects are dim, or credit card debt is piling up, sometimes you need some divine intervention. There are two ways magic can help.

Heart and dollar sign graffiti for how to make a money spell article on the numinous

First, you perform a simple spell, ceremony or ritual intended to make you more charming, articulate and commanding, in order to land a new job or client. To do this, simply write a description of your ideal self, i.e.: "I am charming, articulate and commanding, and my talents are highly valued". Now light a green candle, feel into the physical sensations of landing you dream job, and then burn your note.

Second, you can consider casting a spell meant to affect the outer world and bring you more wealth – but you should only try this approach if working on yourself hasn't solved the problem!

– Go for a walk in a busy area—ideally a place of commerce—and collect 13 lucky pennies. A lucky penny is any penny you find that's facing up. Any pennies you find facing down, you should turn over and leave for someone else. In a pinch, you can use dimes, nickels or quarters, but whatever you choose, you should not mix and match. You might need to take several walks!

– Put the lucky coins in a suitable container like a glass mason jar, and fill it with water. You can dress it by adding a combination of these common household herbs: cinnamon, thyme, basil, cloves and ginger. You can pick a few or just one, whatever you have to hand.

– Seal the jar by screwing the lid on tight and burning a green candle atop it. Meditate as you do so, visualizing yourself enjoying the wealth you're about to receive.

– On the night of the Full Moon, bury the container in the earth in a place it won't be disturbed. On the dirt above it, draw a pentagram with the top pointing west.

If you can't get out into nature to bury your spell properly, here's an alternative method:

Instead of filling the jar of pennies with water, fill it with dirt. You can collect the dirt from outside or use a small packet of soil. You could also use sand from the beach or fill it up with rocks. Dress the dirt with the same herbs mentioned above. Seal the jar with a green candle, do your meditation, and then you can leave the spell on your altar.

When the spell is no longer relevant, you should still take it out somewhere in nature and bury it, drawing a westward facing pentagram on the soil above. This act seals your spell, planting a seed of wealth that will grow over time. Generally, you don't really want to dispose of the spell by emptying the contents of the jar, as that might adversely affect your future finances.

Try this money spell to boost your finances, level up your career, or to bail you out in tough times – but remember to start by first casting the twin spells of gratitude and generosity. Then attempt spells directed at improving yourself and enhancing your innate talents. Only reach to the Money Jar spell when nothing else does seem to be doing the trick.

FREE MAGIC BUSINESS SPELLS, INCANTATIONS, AND RITUALS

Business spells, often referred to as success spells, are magic spells designed to assist with business endeavors. They are easy spells and simple to work. They are good for newly established or older businesses to increase profits and bring prosperity.

Business Spell

To attract customers-

You will need:

-a small jar with a lid

Equal shares of-

-Myrrh

-Mimosa

-Jasmine

-Patchouli

Mix all of these ingredients well in the jar and place the lid on the jar.

Each morning, prior to the opening of your store or shop, rub the door handles with this preparation.

Business Success Spell

This spell requires a small stone. The spell works best with a bloodstone, malachite, or green tourmaline, but any stone can work.

Hold your selected stone in your left hand during a full moon.

In your mind's eye, visualize money flowing into your business using whatever images work best for you: customers handing you large amounts of money, your mailbox filling up with orders, or your next bank statement showing a huge increase. The image should take the incoming flow to the extreme, don't hold back on this part of the spell.

While you are picturing this rush of cash, speak the following words aloud:

Money comes and money grows

Quickly in the money flows

Fill my coffers to the top, ever higher, never stop.

Place the stone in your pocket or purse and carry it with you at all times.

SPELL FOR PROFESSIONAL SUCCESS

This Wiccan spell for professional success can be used for a few purposes:

- To get a job to increase your salary to start a new business
- To increase the success of your current business

Ingredients of white magic success spell

- A photo of yourself
- 4 green spell candles and one white spell candle
- A few drops of essential oil for your astrological sign Amber incense 10 bay leaves 2 green fluorite crystals or orgonite containing fluorite Money
- A note of any denomination will do

An offering bowl Dress in white when you perform this spell.

Purify yourself by washing your hands and then applying a few drops of your essential oil (mix a drop with a carrier oil such as almond oil, as many essential oils can irritate the skin if put on the skin directly)

To prepare your circle, place the green candles at each cardinal point, and the white candle in front of you.

Place the incense to the left of the white candle.

Put the bay leaves, fluorite stones and the bank note into a bowl, and put this on the right of the white candle.

Put your photo in front of the candle. Now, ground and center yourself, then draw your circle, lighting each green candle in turn, and finally the white candle in front of you. Use the white candle to light the incense.

Take the white candle, and drop a few drops of wax on your picture.

Take the offering bowl in both hands and concentrate on your photo.

Recite this incantation for personal success three times:

"Success is coming soon to me, Prosperity is flowing unto me, so must it be"

Now sit in silence for a while and visualize having complete financial freedom. Money is flowing easily to you – you are in total flow and abundance.

Imagine what that would be like.

Immerse yourself in the feeling of it.

The longer you can hold this happy image in your mind, the better. When you feel done, extinguish all candles ending with the white candle.

Close the circle and let the incense burn to the end. Afterwards, whenever you think of money or professional success, remember the happy feelings of the abundance visualization, and get into that feeling again. If you find yourself worrying, immediately recite the above incantation, and refocus your thoughts towards abundance, knowing that the more you think positively about your future success, the quicker you will draw it into your life.

Made in the USA
Las Vegas, NV
18 January 2022